USBORNE

Write-in

PLANET EARTH

Activity Book

Written by Lizzie Cope and Sam Baer

Illustrated by Ruaida Mannaa, Josy Bloggs, Brittany Baugus and Giulia Lombardo

Designed by Samuel Gorham, Jamie Ball and Jacqui Clark

Edited by James Maclaine

EXPLORE PLANET EARTH

This book will take you on an amazing journey around the world. Check what lies ahead in the contents below.

Here's what the Earth looks like from space...

NORTH AMERICA

Did you know that clouds of dust cross the Atlantic? Turn to page 30 to see where from.

PACIFIC OCEAN

SOUTH AMERICA

N
W E
S

ANTARCTICA

CONTENTS

4-5	Inside and outside the Earth	24-25	Frozen forests
6-7	Difficult deserts	26-27	The Ring of Fire
8-9	Wonderful waterfalls	28-29	Deep underground
10-11	Sky-scraping mountains	30-31	Extreme weather
12-13	Surging seas	32-33	Record-breaking landmarks
14-15	All sorts of cities	34-35	The Grand Canyon
16-17	The greatest journeys on Earth	36-37	Islands in the seas
18-19	Tangled mangroves	38-39	Sprawling savannahs
20-21	The icy north and south	40-41	River race
22-23	The amazing Amazon	42-43	Deep underwater

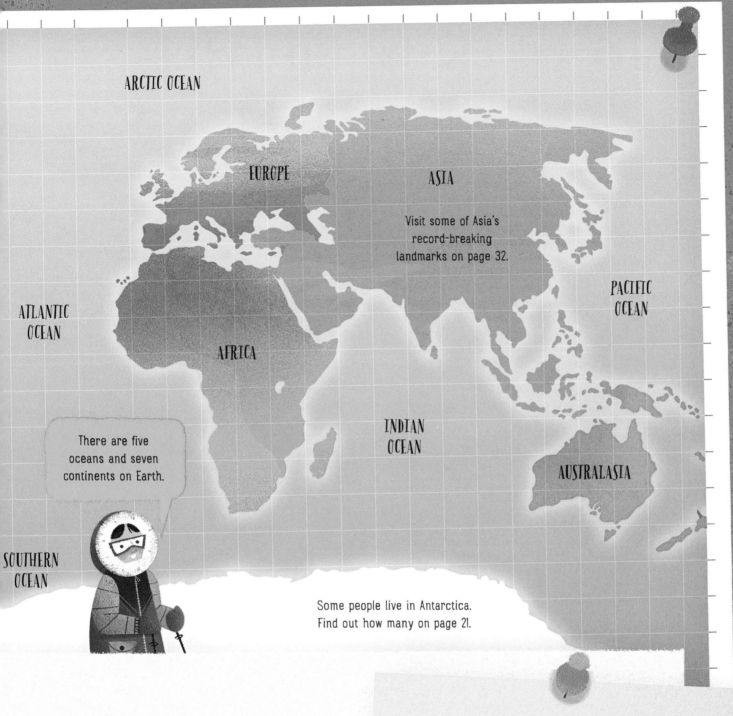

ARCTIC OCEAN

EUROPE

ASIA

Visit some of Asia's
record-breaking
landmarks on page 32.

PACIFIC
OCEAN

ATLANTIC
OCEAN

AFRICA

INDIAN
OCEAN

AUSTRALASIA

There are five
oceans and seven
continents on Earth.

SOUTHERN
OCEAN

Some people live in Antarctica.
Find out how many on page 21.

44-45	Feeding the planet
46-47	The Great Lakes
48-49	The Great Barrier Reef
50-51	Quaking Earth
52-53	World of wonders
54-55	Tortoise islands
56-57	Looking up from Earth
58-59	Save the planet
60	Spread the word
61-64	Answers and solutions

Usborne Quicklinks

For links to websites where you can find out
EVEN MORE about Planet Earth, with puzzles,
games and test-yourself quizzes, plus ways
to help the planet, go to

usborne.com/Quicklinks

and type in the title of this book.

Please follow the internet safety guidelines
at Usborne Quicklinks. Children should be
supervised online.

INSIDE AND OUTSIDE THE EARTH

Planet Earth is not absolutely round. It's shaped like a slightly squashed ball. Discover what it's made of – both above and below its surface – as you solve all these puzzles...

Surface spotting

Can you locate these close-up views of the planet on the big globe opposite?

A.
B.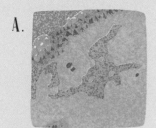

C.
D.

E.
F.

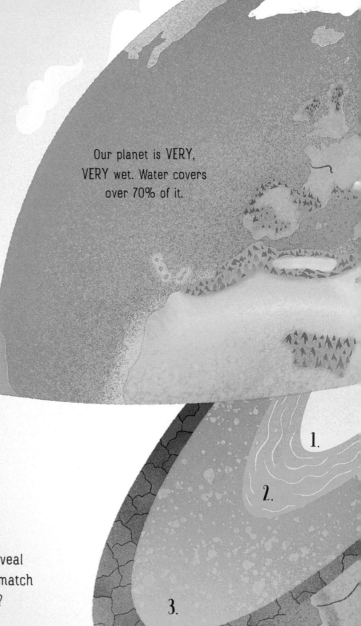

Our planet is VERY, VERY wet. Water covers over 70% of it.

1.

2.

3.

4.

Hidden layers

If you could cut a giant wedge out of the Earth to reveal what's inside, you'd see four different layers. Can you match the names to the numbers using the descriptions?

○ **Mantle**
The thickest layer is a mixture of rock and metal.

○ **Crust**
This rocky layer floats on top of the mantle.

○ **Inner core**
This part is solid. It's made up of the metals iron and nickel.

○ **Outer core**
The metals here are liquid.

Up in the air

The Earth is surrounded by different layers of gases. They make up the atmosphere, which protects the planet against the Sun's powerful rays.

These labels show the names of the five main layers – and how far each one is from Earth.

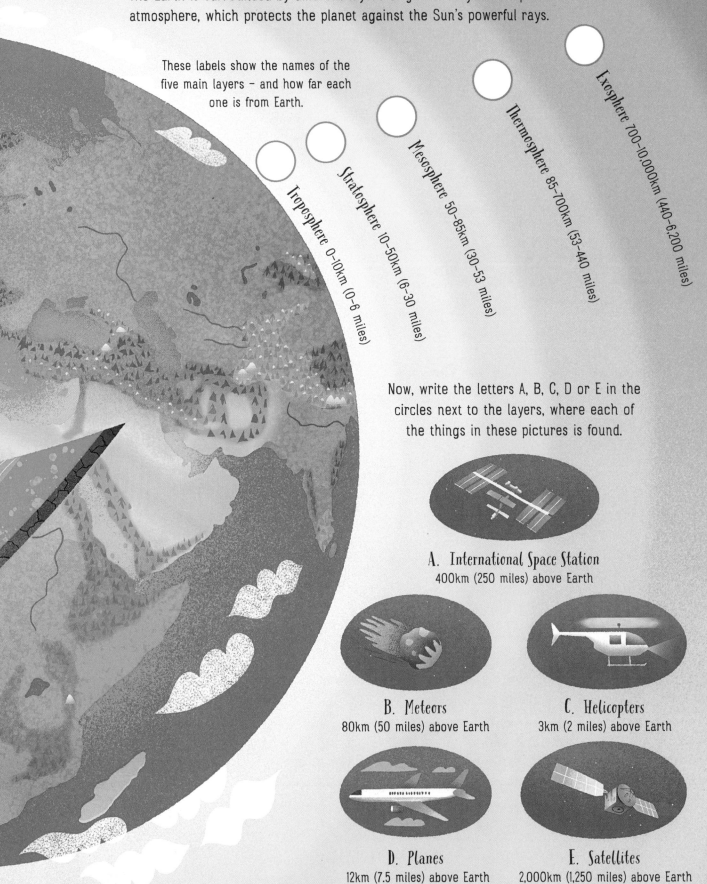

Troposphere 0–10km (0–6 miles)

Stratosphere 10–50km (6–30 miles)

Mesosphere 50–85km (30–53 miles)

Thermosphere 85–700km (53–440 miles)

Exosphere 700–10,000km (440–6,200 miles)

Now, write the letters A, B, C, D or E in the circles next to the layers, where each of the things in these pictures is found.

A. International Space Station
400km (250 miles) above Earth

B. Meteors
80km (50 miles) above Earth

C. Helicopters
3km (2 miles) above Earth

D. Planes
12km (7.5 miles) above Earth

E. Satellites
2,000km (1,250 miles) above Earth

DIFFICULT DESERTS

With extreme temperatures and very little rainfall, deserts test
the skills of animals and plants to survive.

Saharan survivors

These creatures all live in the Sahara Desert in northern Africa.
Can you draw lines to link each one to its description?

1. Sandfish

2. Fennec fox

3. Saharan silver ant

4. Addax

A. Its shiny body helps to reflect heat.

B. Flat, wide hooves allow it to walk on soft sand.

C. Big ears keep it cool.

D. It escapes sunlight by wiggling through sand.

Count the arms

In the Sonoran Desert in North America, plants called saguaro cacti store water in their stems. When they're about 70 years old, they start growing arms to keep extra water. The more arms a cactus has, the older it is. Can you write numbers above these cacti, to put them in order from youngest to oldest?

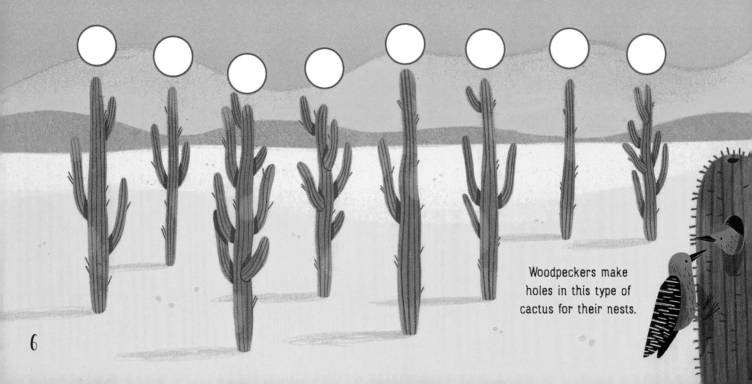

Woodpeckers make holes in this type of cactus for their nests.

Desert bloom

The Atacama Desert in South America is one of the driest places in the world. BUT if it ever rains, lots of plants suddenly burst into flower.

Can you find these five squares in the big picture?

Example:

1.

C2

2.

3.

4.

5.

From flower to flower

Hungry bees and butterflies rush to feed on the desert flowers' sweet nectar. They also carry pollen between the plants. This helps them to make seeds, which will grow into new plants.

Follow each trail to find out which insect visited the most flowers.

A.

B.

C.

D.

E.

7

WONDERFUL WATERFALLS

This picture shows part of the ENORMOUS Iguazú Falls in South America.
Can you spot its name hidden in the cascades – along with nineteen other
breathtaking waterfalls from around the world?

Waterfall search

Find all the names, shown in **bold** below, in
the grids of letters. They might go up, down,
across, diagonally, forwards or backwards.

1. **Niagara** Falls (North America)
2. **Gullfoss** Falls (Europe)
3. **Angel** Falls (South America)
4. **Tugela** Falls (Africa)
5. **Sutherland** Falls (Australasia)
6. **Nachi** Falls (Asia)
7. **Havasu** Falls (North America)
8. **Wallaman** Falls (Australasia)
9. **Kaieteur** Falls (South America)
10. **Khone Phapheng** Falls (Asia)
11. **Iguazú** Falls (South America)
12. **Yosemite** Falls (North America)
13. **Reichenbach** Falls (Europe)
14. **Barron** Falls (Australasia)
15. **Kalambo** Falls (Africa)
16. **Victoria** Falls (Africa)
17. **Rhine** Falls (Europe)
18. **Inga** Falls (Africa)
19. **Dip** Falls (Australasia)
20. **Jog** Falls (Asia)

> Victoria Falls is also
> known as Mosi-oa-Tunya.

```
O V W Q                 L O M
J P L R             D G Y P O
C N S W A           A I S V Z
J G W E Z I         U M O V L A N
J S E Z R           O C B L W R
S L K P O           E G H M Y D A
P L N T             P C D A B V G
D E R C             Q P S L N L A
D T F S I           F U Z A U G I
U T V               H N K U B A A
                    Q W G A Z
                        L E

V R O A H
G T M J E N
C U S V N I                 S
U L D N S                   N
K B L A             T I L
L G P F             H A Y D
I P D A O           T J G N B
O M L I A S H M E A W I
T S P E L T J S O L R F G
U I W A L L A M A N D
```

Record breakers

Four waterfalls from the list above
hold world records. Read these
clues, then write numbers in the
circles to identify them.

Fastest-flowing waterfall
It's the only African waterfall
in the list that has the
letter N in its name.

Widest waterfall
The letter H appears three
times in its name.

Spot the swifts

Nimble-winged birds called great dusky swifts dart behind the water to build their nests. How many birds can you spot flying around the falls?

Great dusky swift nest

Tallest waterfall
The letters in its name can be rearranged to spell GLEAN.

Biggest sheet of falling water
Britain's queen between 1837 and 1901 shares one of its names.

SKY-SCRAPING MOUNTAINS

The dizzyingly high peaks of the highest mountains on every continent are described as the Seven Summits.

Higher and higher

Can you identify which is which? Read the clues on the opposite page and write the numbers 1-7 in the circles for your answers.

1. Aconcagua
(South America)

2. Denali
(North America)

3. Mount Elbrus
(Europe)

4. Mount Kilimanjaro
(Africa)

5. Mount Everest
(Asia)

6. Mount Vinson
(Antarctica)

7. Puncak Jaya
(Australasia)

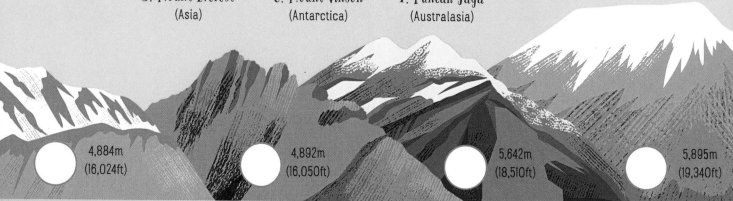

4,884m
(16,024ft)

4,892m
(16,050ft)

5,642m
(18,510ft)

5,895m
(19,340ft)

Back to the woods

Forests on DENALI are home to black bears. Can you find this bear's den?

Denali's upper slopes are too cold for trees to survive. The point where trees stop growing is called the TREE LINE.

It's in a group of trees that looks like this.

CLUES

▲ Africa has a taller mountain than Europe.

▲ The highest mountain in Australasia is just 8m (26ft) taller than the one in Antarctica.

▲ Denali's peak is over 6,000m (19,685ft) high.

▲ Aconcagua is 1,890m (6,200ft) shorter than Mount Everest – the world's highest mountain.

Everest is getting EVEN TALLER. It's growing about 0.5cm (0.2 inches) every year.

6,190m (20,310ft)

6,959m (22,831ft)

8,849m (29,031ft)

Cold at the top

It gets colder and colder the higher you go up a mountain. Can you work out where each temperature was recorded on MOUNT KILIMANJARO? Compare the key with the mountain and thermometer pictures, then write the letters A–F in the circles.

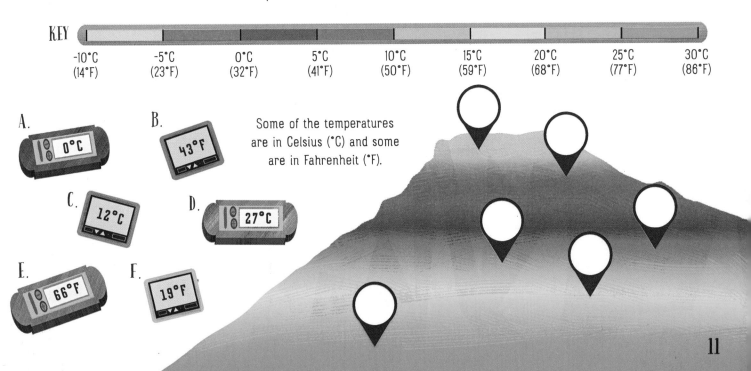

KEY

-10°C (14°F)   -5°C (23°F)   0°C (32°F)   5°C (41°F)   10°C (50°F)   15°C (59°F)   20°C (68°F)   25°C (77°F)   30°C (86°F)

A. 0°C

B. 43°F

Some of the temperatures are in Celsius (°C) and some are in Fahrenheit (°F).

C. 12°C

D. 27°C

E. 66°F

F. 19°F

SURGING SEAS

The water in all the world's oceans and seas NEVER stops moving.
That's because of waves, currents and tides.

Big waves

Jaw-droppingly TALL waves sometimes rise up without warning and dwarf all the other waves around them. They're known as rogue waves.

Can you find the words ROGUE WAVE hidden somewhere in these rows of letters? Underline the words when you spot them.

RUEGOWVAEORGE
OUEGRVAEWRUGEOWVAE
GROEUEVAWRGUOEEWAVUR
REUGOAWVEGROEUAVERO
WORRUEAGOUEVAVAEWRU
WOGRUEAVOUEGRVAEWRUG
REUGOAWVEGROEUAVEROU
WOGRUEAVOUEGRVAEWRUGE
REUGOAWVEGROEUAVEROGEU
RWOGRUEAVOUEGRVAEWRUGEO
REUGOAWVEGROGUEWAVEROGERO
RWOGRUEAVOUEGRVAEWRUGEWAVREO

Scientists have measured rogue waves in the Indian Ocean as high as buildings, ten floors tall.

Lost city

When waves CRASH against rocky coastlines, they gradually wear them away. Historians think that this caused the ancient Egyptian city Thonis-Heracleion to sink beneath the Mediterranean Sea over a thousand years ago.

Amazingly, the city's remains are still there for divers to explore. How many of each of these objects can you spot?

Gold coins ....

Statues ....

Clay pots ....

Track the ducks

In 1992, thousands of rubber ducks fell off a container ship in the Pacific Ocean and drifted ALL around the world... but how? They were carried by ocean currents – streams of seawater flowing in different directions. Follow the lines on this map to find out which duck ended up where.

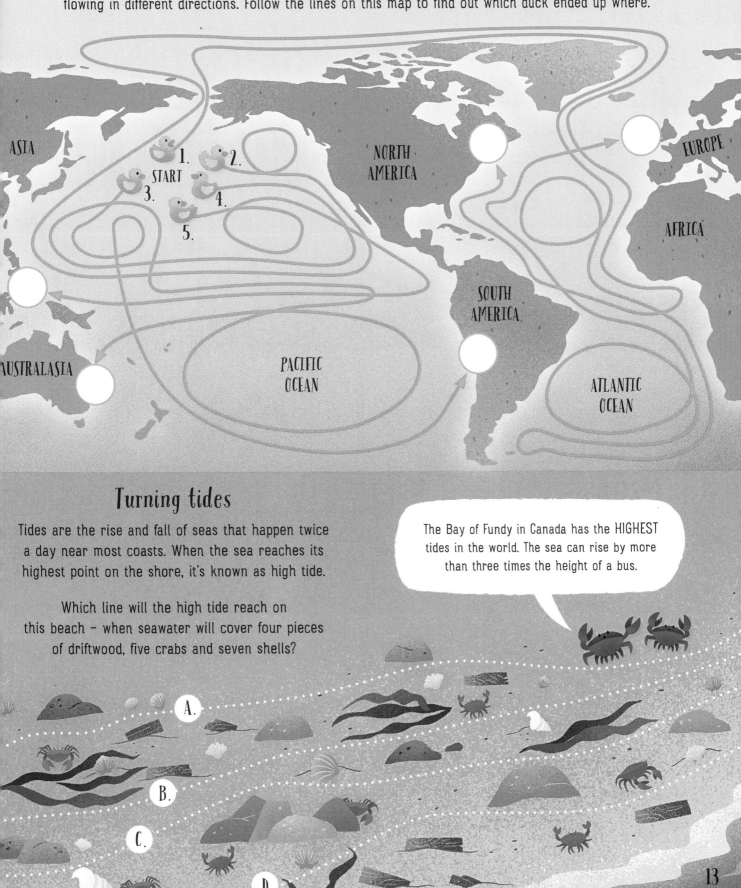

ASIA

NORTH AMERICA

EUROPE

AFRICA

START
1. 2. 3. 4. 5.

SOUTH AMERICA

AUSTRALASIA

PACIFIC OCEAN

ATLANTIC OCEAN

Turning tides

Tides are the rise and fall of seas that happen twice a day near most coasts. When the sea reaches its highest point on the shore, it's known as high tide.

Which line will the high tide reach on this beach – when seawater will cover four pieces of driftwood, five crabs and seven shells?

The Bay of Fundy in Canada has the HIGHEST tides in the world. The sea can rise by more than three times the height of a bus.

A.

B.

C.

D.

ALL SORTS OF CITIES

From ancient forts to busy ports, skyscraper-packed streets to leafy avenues,
bustling cities are home to more than half the people on Earth.

Skyline shapes

Can you match these pictures of six different cities to the labels below them?

A.

B.

C.

D.

E.

F.

○ **Tampa, The US**
has more trees than any
other city.

○ **Cape Town, South Africa**
is near the flat-topped
Table Mountain.

○ **Manila, Philippines**
has lots of skyscrapers.

○ **Carcassonne, France**
is protected by fortress walls.

○ **La Paz, Bolivia**
has the world's largest
cable car system.

○ **Sydney, Australia**
is on the coast.

Build a city

Now, draw your own city skyline.

You could copy some of the shapes from the pictures above, or use your imagination.

Two-wheel tour

Copenhagen in Denmark is one of the world's most eco-friendly cities. Because there are more bikes than cars on its roads, it's sometimes called the City of Cyclists.

Can you guide the cyclist on the red bike to Queen Louise's Bridge? Draw a route that visits all these places, in the order they're listed below, without using the same road TWICE.

1. Little Mermaid Statue
2. Gefion Fountain
3. National Gallery of Denmark
4. Frederik's Church
5. Nyhavn
6. Christiansborg Palace
7. Tivoli Gardens
8. Round Tower
9. Rosenborg Castle
10. Botanical Gardens

Wind power provides much of the city's electricity.

Green spaces cover 25% of Copenhagen.

Little Mermaid Statue

National Gallery of Denmark

Queen Louise's Bridge

Botanical Gardens

Frederik's Church

Gefion Fountain

Rosenborg Castle

Round Tower

Nyhavn

This water is kept clean for swimming.

Some buildings even have plants growing on their roofs.

COPENHAGEN

Tivoli Gardens

Christiansborg Palace

THE GREATEST JOURNEYS ON EARTH

At different times of the year, animals travel great distances by land, air or sea,
in search of food, better weather and places to have their babies.
Their INCREDIBLE journeys are known as migrations.

On the move

Herds of animals follow the rainy season across Kenya and
Tanzania, in east Africa, to find fresh grass.

Are there more gazelles, zebras or wildebeest in this big picture?

....

Gazelle   Zebra   Wildebeest

Tracking birds

Read about these birds' migrations, then label each
picture A, B or C, to show how far you think it flies.

Arctic terns escape the
dark Arctic winter and fly all
the way to Antarctica at the
other end of the planet.

Blue grouse migrate down
from the Rocky Mountains
in the US, to make their
nests in the valleys below.

Eurasian cranes fly across
Europe in winter, migrating from
Finland in the north to Spain
in the south.

A. 300m (1,000ft)   B. 4,000km (2,500 miles)   C. 24,000km (15,000 miles)

Watch out! Big cats follow the migration to hunt any weak animals. How many leopards can you spot?

Lost fawns

Baby animals have to keep up with the rest of the herd.

Can you guide these gazelle fawns to their mothers on this page? The patterns on each fawn and its mother match.

Against the flow

Tens of thousands of salmon migrate from the Atlantic Ocean to swim up rivers in Scotland, where they lay their eggs. Can you circle the six salmon swimming the wrong way?

TANGLED MANGROVES

Have you heard of mangroves? These UNUSUAL trees grow in saltwater swamps across southeast Asia. They have jumbled, stilt-like roots that filter out salt and support the trunks and branches above the water's surface.

Protective plants

How many fish are hiding from the crocodile in these mangrove roots?

....

A.

B.

C.

Whose roots?

Follow these roots back to the trunks, to find out which tree each one connects to. Write in the letter for each answer.

1.

2.

3.

Plastic problem

Too much plastic ends up in the world's seas and some gets trapped in mangroves.

How many sacks do these volunteers need to clear away all the plastic?
Each sack can hold five bottles or ten blue bags.

.... sacks

Plastic waste harms
the trees and animals
that live here.

Mini mangroves

Volunteers also plant trees to help
mangroves to survive. Can you draw some
baby trees in this part of the swamp?

THE ICY NORTH AND SOUTH

Brrrrrr! The Arctic Ocean around the top of the Earth is cold enough to freeze in winter. At the opposite end of the planet is Antarctica – an entire continent covered in ice and snow.

Cracks in the ice

Polar bears trek long distances across the frozen Arctic in search of food. But in the summer months, the ice starts to melt... and crack!

Can you draw a route for this polar bear, avoiding all the cracks?

Planet Earth is getting warmer, so Arctic sea ice is melting earlier each year. This means there are fewer and fewer places where polar bears can hunt.

FINISH

Tip of the iceberg

Giant blocks of ice, called icebergs, float in the Arctic and around Antarctica. Hidden beneath the surface, the lower part of an iceberg is EVEN bigger.

Can you fill in the squares to complete each iceberg? The bottom needs to be SEVEN times bigger than the top.

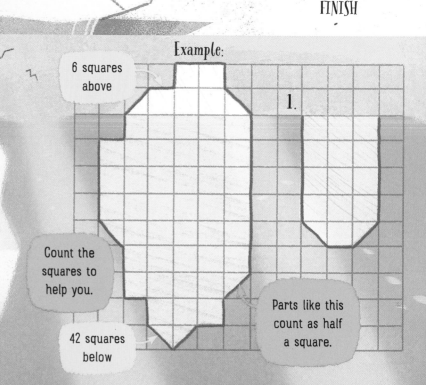

Example:

6 squares above

1.

Count the squares to help you.

42 squares below

Parts like this count as half a square.

20

Southern stations

There are no towns in Antarctica, but there are research stations where scientists live and work for months at a time. This map shows some of the research stations and the number of scientists based at each one.

Can you find the South Pole – the southernmost point on Earth? Follow the instructions on the right.

INSTRUCTIONS

First, look for the two places with the BIGGEST and SMALLEST numbers of scientists – and draw a straight line between them.

Then, draw another line between two stations, where one has twice as many scientists as the other.

The South Pole is where the two lines cross.

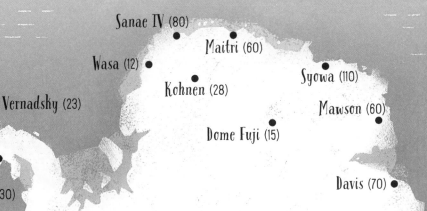

Sanae IV (80)

Maitri (60)

Wasa (12)

Syowa (110)

Kohnen (28)

Vernadsky (23)

Mawson (60)

Dome Fuji (15)

Rothera (130)

Davis (70)

Vostok (25)

Mirny (169)

Concordia (60)

Casey (65)

McMurdo (1,000)

Mario Zucchelli (90)

Dumont d'Urville (100)

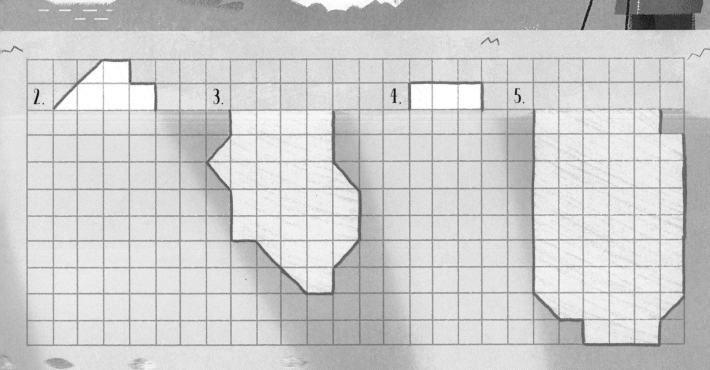

2.   3.   4.   5.

THE AMAZING AMAZON

Forests that grow in warm, wet places are called tropical rainforests. The Amazon Rainforest is the LARGEST in the world and covers more than a QUARTER of South America.

Emergent layer
This is where the tips of the tallest trees poke through.

Canopy
Leafy treetops overlap each other to make a shady canopy.

Layers of life

Like all rainforests, the Amazon is made up of four different layers. Which of these creatures can you NOT spot among them?

three emerald tree boas

three sword-billed hummingbirds

two howler monkeys

a giant anteater

a matamata turtle

two scarlet macaws

two jaguars

two malachite butterflies

a leaf-mimic katydid

The under canopy
Small trees and shrubs grow here.

Forest floor
Twisted roots and old leaves carpet the ground.

What's that flower?

Scientists visit the Amazon to study all its different wildlife and plants. Can you help this scientist identify the flowers in the pictures? Write numbers under them to show which one's which.

Draw an X in the circle that's left. Maybe I've discovered a new type of orchid?

1. Dracula orchid
   – triangular flower with blood-red tips

2. Masdevallia orchid
   – pink flower with three long, thin tubes

3. Aganisia orchid
   – white flower with a yellow middle

4. Pescatoria orchid
   – white flower with pink edges

5. Cleistes orchid
   – pink and yellow flower

Monkey maze

Every year, huge numbers of trees are cut down for wood or burned to clear space for farmland. Can you help these spider monkeys reach a different part of the forest? They must follow the treetops to keep safe.

If people don't stop destroying the Amazon, spider monkeys and MILLIONS more living things will lose their homes forever.

END

START

FROZEN FORESTS

About one third of ALL the trees on Earth are found in snow-covered forests called taigas.
They stretch across the north of the planet in parts of Asia, Europe and North America.

Tough trees

Only cold-hardy trees grow
in taigas, such as...

Spruce   Pine   Larch

How many of each type can you
count in the big scene?

Beware of the bogs

Can you guide this reindeer rider
through the trees and back to the camp?
The reindeer can't step on boggy ground
– or it might sink.

Bog

Taiga tiger

Can you spot a Siberian tiger – the biggest type of cat in the world? It's lurking somewhere on these pages...

Camp

Camp conversation

The Evenki people live in Siberia, in Russia. Their tents are known as chums (say *chooms*). Can you work out what each person below is saying in Evenki? Write the letters A, B, C or D in the circle next to each correct translation.

A.
On bidieres?

B.
Bi sot depmulim.

C.
Orochi-gu bihinni?

D.
Bihin, iyeye achin. Bihin, er – iyeye achin.

Yes, this one – without antlers. ◯

How are you? ◯

I'm so hungry. ◯

Do you have reindeer? ◯

25

THE RING OF FIRE

Beware of the Ring of Fire! This name describes the edges of the Pacific Ocean, where at least 75% of the world's volcanoes are found.

Mapping volcanoes

Read the clues below, then write the letters A–F on the map, to identify six volcanoes in the Ring of Fire.

CLUES

A. **Tarawera** is in Australasia.

B. **Pinatubo** is the furthest west of the six.

C. **Mount St. Helens** is in North America.

D. **Michinmahuida** is southeast of Tarawera.

E. **Mount Fuji** is closest to Pinatubo.

F. **El Jorullo** is southeast of Mount St. Helens.

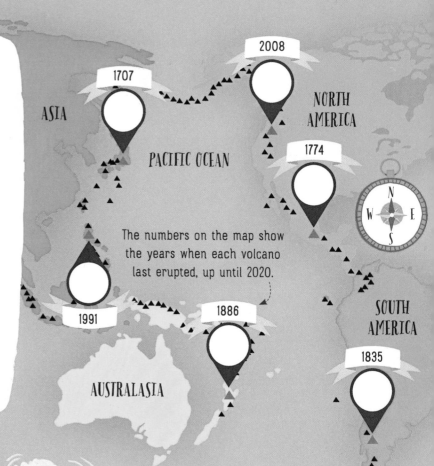

The numbers on the map show the years when each volcano last erupted, up until 2020.

ASIA · PACIFIC OCEAN · NORTH AMERICA · SOUTH AMERICA · AUSTRALASIA

1707 · 2008 · 1774 · 1991 · 1886 · 1835

Timeline

Volcanoes shoot out hot ash, gases and liquid rock called lava when they erupt. Can you add the letters A–F to this timeline, to put the dates of the same six volcanoes' last eruptions in order?

Volcanoes that haven't erupted for some time – but might erupt again – are described as dormant. This means they're sleeping.

1700 1720 1740 1760 1780 1800 1820 1840 1860 1880 1900 1920 1940 1960 1980 2000 2020

Eruption report

In 1980, Mount St. Helens had its first major eruption in over a hundred years.

Can you fill in the five details missing from this newspaper report?

ash

sky

stream

speed

8:32am

BREAKING NEWS: DISASTER STRIKES

Mount St. Helens erupted this morning at .... An enormous cloud of .... blasted out of the volcano and shot 26km (16 miles) straight up into the ....

Next, the volcano released its pyroclastic flow: a .... of rock, gas and ash that raced along the ground.

The flow reached a top .... of 130km/h (80mph) and temperatures as high as 700°C (1,300°F).

Race to the top

Some dormant volcanoes are safe enough to visit – and even climb. This picture shows three routes to the top of Mount Fuji – and how many hours and minutes the different sections take to complete.

Can you add up the total time for each route? Then, circle the one this climber should choose, to reach the top as fast as she can.

A. __ hours __ minutes

B. __ hours __ minutes

C. __ hours __ minutes

2 hours

1 hour 45 minutes

1 hour 30 minutes

2 hours 15 minutes

2 hours 15 minutes

1 hour 15 minutes

2 hours 30 minutes

3 hours 45 minutes

2 hours 30 minutes

A.

B.

C.

27

DEEP UNDERGROUND

It's time to head beneath the Earth's surface,
to explore the secret world of caves...

Bat naps

Copy the shapes to fill this cave with bats sleeping
upside down – and fluttering around, too.

Inside some caves, tiny amounts of
rock dissolve in dripping water, then
harden again. This makes spiny rocks
that hang down – called stalactites...

...and stalagmites
that point up.

Strange names

These weirdly beautiful rocks are also
found in caves. Can you draw lines to
link the labels to the pictures?

Cave popcorn   Cave bacon

Cave frostwork   Soda straws

Crystal cave

In the year 2000, miners searching for silver in Mexico discovered
a cave like no other on Earth. It was full of GIANT crystals.
Can you find your way to the bottom right corner?

START HERE.

These crystals grew
in mineral-rich water
that filled the cave
– until the miners
pumped it dry.

END

EXTREME WEATHER

Whoosh, splash, crash! Brace yourself for some of the WILDEST weather on Earth – from globetrotting dust clouds to never-ending lightning storms.

Drifting dust

When gusty winds blow across the Sahara Desert in Africa, they whip up dust into the air. Clouds of this dust then drift west to places as far away as Cuba, on the other side of the Atlantic Ocean.

Can you peer through the haze to identify the little picture that shows EXACTLY the same scene before the dust cloud arrived?

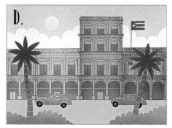

Wet season sudoku

A staggering 75% of the rain that falls in India each year happens between June and September. Downpours in these months can flood towns and cities – but they also fill fields with water, where farmers grow rice.

Can you draw lines for rice plants in the grid? There should be one, two, three, four, five and six rice plants in every row, column and different blue block of squares.

How much hail?

Kericho in Kenya is best known for two things: tea farms and hailstorms. Add up the numbers on all the hailstones to find out how many days of hail Kericho can have in a year.

10

5

10

5

15

5

10

5

18

2

5

Not again!

20

22

.... days

Lots of lightning

Lake Maracaibo in Venezuela is the lightning capital of the world. Storms rage above the lake almost EVERY day, firing out over a million lightning bolts in a year.

Doodle lightning to fill the sky.

RECORD-BREAKING LANDMARKS

These stamps are inspired by the biggest, tallest and oldest structures on Earth — and some other record holders, too. Use pencils or felt-tip pens to brighten them all.

TALLEST STATUE

Statue of Unity, India
Height: 182m (597ft)

Capital Gate **UAE**

FURTHEST LEANING SKYSCRAPER

LARGEST TELESCOPE

Gran Telescopio Canarias, Spain

GREAT PYRAMID OF GIZA, EGYPT

TALLEST BUILDING OF THE ANCIENT WORLD

Oldest Ferris wheel
1897
Riesenrad, Austria

LARGEST CASTLE

MALBORK CASTLE, POLAND

Makkah Royal Clock Tower
Saudi Arabia

LARGEST CLOCK FACE

Largest indoor rainforest

EDEN PROJECT
UK

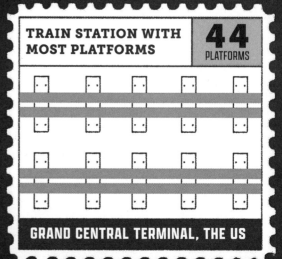

TRAIN STATION WITH MOST PLATFORMS

44 PLATFORMS

GRAND CENTRAL TERMINAL, THE US

NIESEN
MOUNTAIN
Switzerland

LONGEST STAIRCASE
11,674 stairs

OLDEST TREEHOUSE
1692
PITCHFORD TREEHOUSE, UK

LARGEST PINEAPPLE-SHAPED BUILDING

17M (56FT) TALL

THE BIG PINEAPPLE
SOUTH AFRICA

DE NOORD, NETHERLANDS
TALLEST WINDMILL 33m (109ft) tall

OLDEST POST OFFICE OPENED IN
1712

SANQUHAR POST OFFICE, UK

FORBIDDEN CITY, CHINA

MOST VISITED LANDMARK
14 million visitors each year

Grand Bazaar, Turkey

OLDEST COVERED MARKET
— BUILT IN **1461** —

WIDEST CONCRETE DOME
43m (142ft) wide
PANTHEON, ITALY

Tower of Hercules, Spain

OLDEST WORKING LIGHTHOUSE
Over 1,800 years old

Wish you were where?
Can you find the stamp that shows the landmark described in this postcard?

Dear Juju,

The weather was cold outside today, but at least it was warm inside the giant greenhouses!
See you soon,

Bea xx

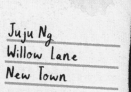

Juju Ng
Willow Lane
New Town

THE GRAND CANYON

There are lots of rocky valleys in the US, but the GRAND CANYON in the state of Arizona is the most impressive of them all. Big enough to be seen from space, it has spectacularly steep sides and stunning views.

Camera angles

Can you work out which of the people below took this picture? Draw straight arrows from their cameras to check the direction they are facing.

Taken by: ....

Charlie

Rosa

Yash

Izzie

Right at the bottom of the canyon is the twisting Colorado River.

Lizard lookout

Can you spot two collared lizards hiding somewhere on these pages? They look like this one.

34

Star spotting

Visitors to the Grand Canyon can see THOUSANDS of stars at night.
That's because there's no light pollution from any cities or towns.

Can you circle the stars and planet that the stargazers below are talking about?

See those three stars in a straight, vertical line? That's Orion's Belt!

The blue star to the right of Orion's Belt is Rigel.

Can you find Venus? It's brighter than everything else.

I'm looking for a red supergiant star called Betelgeuse.

ISLANDS IN THE SEAS

From huge countries to deserted rocks, there are MILLIONS OF ISLANDS on Earth.
In fact, there are SO MANY that no one knows the exact number.

Largest islands

The pictures below show the seven largest islands in the world. Each circle
inside the shapes represents the same-sized area of land.

Greenland is as big as THREE of the other islands combined.
Can you fill in and count all the circles, to help you identify which three?

Sumatra
(Indian Ocean)
....

Every circle is
approximately 50,000km^2
(19,000 square miles).

Baffin Island
(Atlantic Ocean)
....

New Guinea
(Pacific Ocean) ....

Honshu
(Pacific Ocean)

Greenland
(Arctic Ocean)
....

Madagascar
(Indian Ocean)
....

Borneo
(Pacific Ocean) ....

Land of lemurs

Some islands are the ONLY places where certain animals live
in the wild. Madagascar, for example, is home to over 100
types of lemurs, including these...

Ring-tailed
lemurs ( )

Sifakas ( )

Aye-ayes ( )

Red ruffed
lemurs ( )

How many of each
type of lemur can you
spot in this picture?
Write the numbers
on the left.

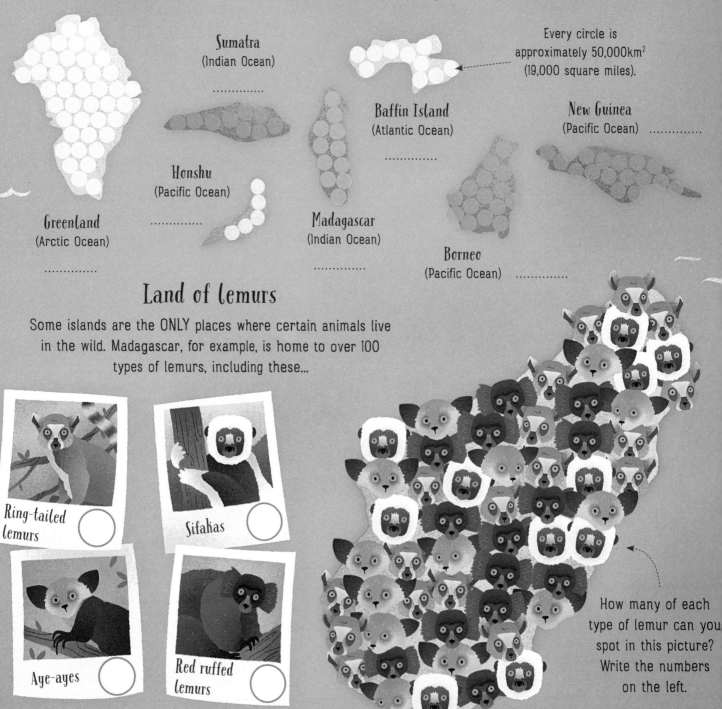

Appearing and disappearing

Did you know that sea levels are rising and swallowing up some islands? Other islands are slowly peeking out of the sea as layers of rocky lava build up from undersea volcanoes.

Can you spot SIX islands that appear or disappear in the second picture?

Artificial islands

Some islands are built by people from scratch. Can you draw lines from the descriptions of four of them to the correct pictures?

1. Swan Island, France
Several bridges over the River Seine in Paris use this island for support.

2. Marker Wadden, Netherlands
This group of islands was created for wildlife in Markermeer Lake.

3. Palm Jumeirah, UAE
Luxury hotels and houses fill this palm-tree-shaped island, off the coast of Dubai.

4. Uros Islands, Peru
The Uros people of Lake Titicaca weave together reeds to make islands that float.

A.

B.

C.

D.

SPRAWLING SAVANNAHS

Savannahs are dry, grassy plains in some warm parts of the world.
They're dotted with trees as far as the eye can see.

Elephant gardeners

African savannah elephants are the largest land animals on Earth. They graze on bushes and trees, which makes room for new plants to grow. Can you reunite this elephant with its herd? It can only go through THREE bushes on the way.

We also help plants by spreading their seeds in our dung.

Connect the dots

Join the numbers from 1 to 105 to reveal a BAOBAB – a strange-looking type of tree that grows in savannahs.

The trunks of baobab trees **BULGE** because they suck up as much water as they can whenever it rains.

Up in flames

KEEP BACK! Grass burns easily when it's dry, so wildfires often happen in savannahs. Only **FOUR** of these facts about wildfires are true. Cross out the two that you think are **FALSE**.

Lightning never causes wildfires.

Some trees grow again after fires.

Wildfires only happen in Australasia.

Some plants only release their seeds during wildfires.

Ash from wildfires helps new plants to grow.

Hawks spread fires so the animals they hunt have nowhere to hide.

RIVER RACE

Set sail down four great rivers from four different continents as you play this game with one or more friends. You'll need one coin each for counters and another coin to flip.

RULES
1. Place your counters on START.
2. Take turns flipping a coin THREE times.
3. Count how many times the coin lands heads up, then move ONE, TWO or THREE spaces along – if you can.
4. The first player to reach END is the winner.

START: ASIA

Mekong River
– home to some of the BIGGEST freshwater fish in the world

Sudd wetland
(South Sudan)

You spot a large bird called a shoebill. Move ahead one space to take a photo.

Strong winds – speed ahead one space.

NEXT CONTINENT: SOUTH AMERICA

The Andes

The Amazon River starts in the Andes Mountains, in Peru.

Stop to watch river dolphins. Skip your next turn.

Amazon River
– the WIDEST river

END

This white-tailed eagle dives in front of you. Go back two spaces.

Go sightseeing. Skip your next turn.

Vienna
(Austria)

Bratislava
(Slovakia)

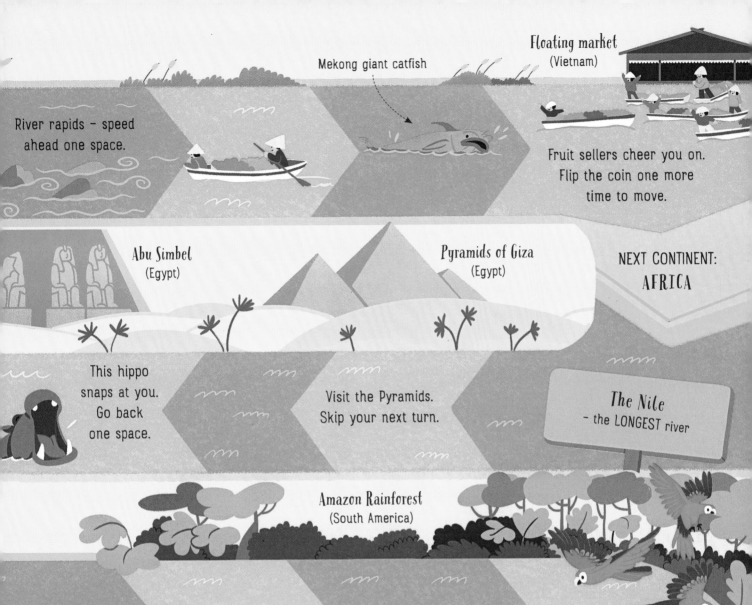

River rapids – speed ahead one space.

Mekong giant catfish

Floating market
(Vietnam)

Fruit sellers cheer you on. Flip the coin one more time to move.

Abu Simbel
(Egypt)

Pyramids of Giza
(Egypt)

NEXT CONTINENT:
AFRICA

This hippo snaps at you. Go back one space.

Visit the Pyramids. Skip your next turn.

The Nile
– the LONGEST river

Amazon Rainforest
(South America)

You've dropped an oar. Go back two spaces to find it.

You spy macaws in the distance. Zoom ahead one space for a closer look.

NEXT CONTINENT:
EUROPE

Tourists in Budapest wish you luck. Flip the coin twice to move again.

The Danube
– the ONLY river to run through four capital cities

Budapest
(Hungary)

Belgrade
(Serbia)

DEEP UNDERWATER

The DEEPEST part of the ocean is at the bottom of the Mariana Trench – a vast crack in the floor of the Pacific. It's 11,034m (36,200ft) below sea level.

Find the trench

The direction of these arrows will lead you to the Mariana Trench's location on the map. Keep drawing the black line, moving one square at a time.

DIRECTIONS

ASIA

AUSTRALASIA

ANTARCTICA

START

Venting letters

Hot water gushes out from the sides of the trench, through chimney-like holes called hydrothermal vents.

Another two-word name for them is hidden in the groups of three letters on the right. For each group, circle the letter that appears first in the alphabet, to spell out the name.

V G	P L	G A	F J	K M
B	Q	R	C	U

W S	N Y	G V	X K	E L	Z R	V W
Z	M	W	P	H	U	S

Name: ....

Glowing in the dark

Not a single ray of sunlight shines this far down, but some of the creatures that live here have bodies that glow. Can you match each pattern of lights to the pictures in the key?

KEY

Deep-sea dragonfish

Black seadevil

Crossota jellyfish

Firefly squid

Hatchetfish

March 26 2012: Mission Log

5:15am: Start of mission. Descended for 2 hours 37 minutes, until...

...........**am**: Reached Challenger Deep. Explored for 3 hours. Then, at...

...........**am**: Left Challenger Deep. Reached the surface after 70 minutes at...

...........**pm**: End of mission.

1.

2.

3.

4.

5.

Journey to the bottom

In 2012, Canadian film director and ocean explorer James Cameron ventured down into the deepest part of the Mariana Trench, known as Challenger Deep. Can you fill in each gap in the mission log with the correct time?

The name of Cameron's submarine was *Deepsea Challenger.*

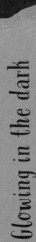

FEEDING THE PLANET

It takes a LOT of food to feed the world's 7.5 billion people. As much as 40% of the land on Earth is used for farms and fields – and rivers, lakes and seas are all fished, too.

Copy cow

There are almost 50 million dairy cows in India and they make over 20% of all the milk in the world.

Can you find the cow with the same pattern of spots as this one?

The great fish escape

Fish farmers in parts of northern Europe keep salmon in large nets as they grow. How many salmon are missing from these nets? There should be 20 in each.

.... salmon have escaped.

SANDI'S SALMON

Collecting cane

Most types of sugar are made from plants called sugar cane. They're grown in tropical countries, such as Brazil. When the canes are ready to harvest, machines cut them down.

Can you write directions and numbers in the gaps on the right, to guide the driver of this machine through all the squares where plants are still growing?

START

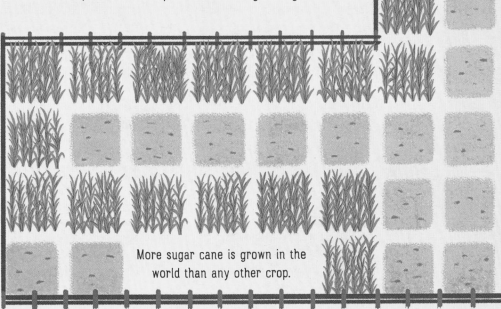

More sugar cane is grown in the world than any other crop.

HARVEST DIRECTIONS

1. Go straight ahead 1 square.
2. Turn left.
3. Go straight ahead .... squares.
4. Turn right.
5. Go straight ahead .... squares.
6. Turn ....
7. Go straight ahead .... squares.
8. Turn ....
9. Go straight ahead .... squares.
10. Turn ....
11. Go straight ahead .... square.

Busy bees

China produces more honey than any other country. Chinese farmers also use honeybees to help crops, such as pear trees and rapeseed plants, make fruit and seeds.

This beekeeper is moving a hive to a new field. Where should it go? Read the rules to find out.

RULES
★ Two hives per field max.
★ No round-shaped hives in fields next to trees.
★ Hives in the same field can't be the same shape.

A.

B.

C.

These rapeseed plants are used to make vegetable oil.

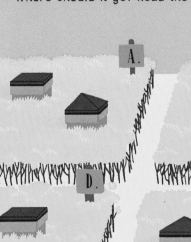

D.

E.

F.

Field ....

THE GREAT LAKES

This map shows the five BIGGEST lakes in North America. Known as the Great Lakes, they contain over 20% of all the fresh water (not salty) on Earth.

Route finder

Find the cities Chicago and Ottawa on the map. Then, draw a route from one to the other, using only the lakes and rivers or canals that connect them.

KEY
● City

The orange land on this map is part of the US. The yellow areas are all in Canada.

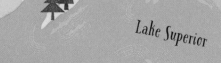
THE US

Lake Superior

Marquette

Lake Michigan

Milwaukee

Chicago

True or false?

Check the map to find the answers to this quiz.

1. Cleveland is on the shore of Lake Superior.
   TRUE / FALSE

2. Lake Michigan is the only Great Lake entirely in the US.
   TRUE / FALSE

3. Detroit is north of Lake Huron.
   TRUE / FALSE

4. Lake Erie is the largest of the Great Lakes.
   TRUE / FALSE

5. Lake Ontario is the furthest east.
   TRUE / FALSE

Superior sketches

Compare these small pictures of Lake Superior to the big one on the map. Can you circle the picture that's the closest match?

A.

B.

C.

D.

Sudbury

Ottawa

CANADA

Kingston

Lake Huron

Toronto

Lake Ontario

Goderich

Rochester

Buffalo

Detroit

Lake Erie

It would take more than a MONTH to cycle around the shores of all the Great Lakes without stopping.

Cleveland

THE GREAT BARRIER REEF

The world's largest system of coral reefs is the Great Barrier Reef, near the east coast of Australia. Each piece of coral that makes up its beautiful, rocky structure is built by THOUSANDS of tiny creatures called polyps.

How many reefs?

Follow the diver's instructions to cross out the numbers on the bubbles. The number left over shows how many coral reefs are part of the Great Barrier Reef.

CROSS OUT...

★ all odd numbers
★ the number of hours in a day
★ numbers ending in 2
★ numbers made up of three digits
★ the number of eyes seven dolphins have
★ the number of sides 1,000 dice have

2,063
364
1,429
3,641
14
180
3,752
2,900
24
6,000
2,112

Coral polyps

Most polyps are smaller than a pea.

Fill in the corals

Did you know that corals turn white when the ocean gets too warm? This is called bleaching and it's very harmful for coral reefs. Luckily, they sometimes recover – if the water cools.

Can you fill in all the white corals on these pages?

Brain coral
Doodle wiggly lines on top, like these.

Flowerpot coral
You could use two shades of pink.

Which fish?

The Great Barrier Reef provides food and shelter for lots of different ocean creatures. Some of them are named after other animals because of the way they look.

Write numbers in the circles next to these four fish, to identify them.

1. Lizardfish

2. Zebra shark

3. Red lionfish

4. Parrotfish

Fan coral
Draw lots of wavy stems.

Staghorn coral
Doodle some spots.

Branch coral
Fill in all the branches so they're red.

If we don't stop ocean temperatures from rising, more and more corals will turn white.

QUAKING EARTH

Enormous sheets of rock – called tectonic plates – move slowly beneath the Earth's surface. The plates rub against each other, causing earthquakes every day. Some earthquakes are devastatingly powerful – BUT most are so gentle that people can't feel them happen.

Plates puzzle

Tectonic plates fit together like a jigsaw puzzle. Can you find the plates below that match these shapes? Write the numbers 1-4 on the map to label them.

1. NAZCA PLATE

2. SCOTIA PLATE

3. PHILIPPINE PLATE

4. ARABIAN PLATE

NORTH AMERICAN PLATE

EURASIAN PLATE

JUAN DE FUCA PLATE

CARIBBEAN PLATE

EURASIAN PLATE

INDIAN PLATE

COCOS PLATE

AFRICAN PLATE

PACIFIC PLATE

AUSTRALIAN PLATE

SOUTH AMERICAN PLATE

AUSTRALIAN PLATE

ANTARCTIC PLATE

The plates on the right of this map connect to those on the left.

Find the faults

The borders between tectonic plates are known as fault lines.
Can you circle the locations of these THREE fault lines on the white lines on the map?

1. San Andreas Fault
links the Juan de Fuca Plate with the Cocos Plate.

2. Mid-Atlantic Ridge
stretches down the western edges of the Eurasian Plate AND the African Plate.

3. Pacific-Antarctic Ridge
is between the Pacific Plate and the Antarctic Plate.

Rippling out

Earthquakes start from a single point, then spread out in every direction at the same speed.

Imagine that an earthquake begins under the pink dot on this map. Can you write the numbers 1-5 in the white circles, to show in which order the earthquake reaches each place below? Check the symbols carefully.

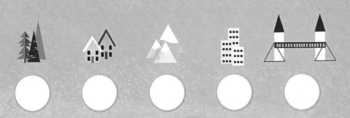

Quake-proof towers

Some incredible buildings have been designed to withstand earthquakes, such as these five skyscrapers. Can you complete their names at the bottom of the page? Find the vowels, A, E, I, O or U, in these two rows of letters. Then write them in the gaps, in the same order, starting on the left.

WRGOMKLEFPEXRONTFGAZSJTOTRVMOREXYSEWAHNKAH

JLIZPOGRELKSDAPQAFLEMITTCAAFWIBUNQWXAGIMLZA

Strong mesh structure

Heavy weights inside the building reduce swaying.

Wide, stable base

T_RR_   T_KY_   SH_NGH_ _ _   TR_NS_M_R_C_   B_RJ

R_F_RM_   SKYTR_ _   T_W_R   PYR_M_D   KH_L_F_

Mexico   Japan   China   The US   UAE

WORLD OF WONDERS

How would you like to visit some of the most spectacular places on Earth? Then take your pick from these locations...

VISIT BLOOD FALLS

There's a waterfall in Antarctica that's BRIGHT RED. Can you guess what makes it look like this?

A. Tiny red plants

B. Lots of iron

C. Molten magma

D. Penguin dung

Look into the world's largest mirror

Salar de Uyuni in Bolivia was once a lake. It dried up a very long time ago, leaving behind a thick layer of salt. When it rains, water transforms the surface into a giant mirror.

Draw the reflections of the Sun, clouds and mountains onto the picture below.

SCALE GIANT STEPS

On the north coast of Northern Ireland, there are thousands of stone columns that were formed by an ancient volcanic eruption. They're known as the Giant's Causeway.

Which column do you reach if you follow the direction of every arrow you come to?

START

MARVEL AT MOUNTAINS

Welcome to Zhangye National Geopark in China. Here you can see rainbow mountains made up of layers of red, blue, yellow and green sandstone. Continue filling in the mountains with different stripes, like this.

TORTOISE ISLANDS

The Galápagos Islands in the Pacific Ocean take their name from an old Spanish word for tortoise. There are GIANT TORTOISES to see here, along with other types of animals found NOWHERE ELSE IN THE WORLD.

Island hopping

Which route on this map of the islands would suit ALL three tourists?

Route ....

ROUTES
A. ● B. ● C. ● D. ●

I want to see tortoises and penguins – but bats scare me.

Can we visit red-footed booby birds?

I'm interested in lizards called marine iguanas.

Pinta

Marchena

Genovesa

Isabela

Santiago

Baltra

Pinzón

Rábida

Santa Cruz   Santa Fé

Fernandina

San Cristóbal

Floreana

Española

Darwin's journey

In 1835, British biologist Charles Darwin visited the Galápagos Islands to study their wildlife. Can you plot the route he took? Starting in the east, he moved clockwise between all the islands with finches on them, like this one.

Real or fake?

One of the Galápagos animals below ISN'T real. Can you match the labels
A–D to the correct pictures, then draw an X in the circle that's left?

A.
This bird dives to the ground to hunt.

B.
This little creature drinks nectar from flowers.

C.
Two wide, webbed feet help this bird to swim.

D.
This furry animal has big front flippers.

○ Galápagos fur seal

○ Galápagos cormorant

○ Galápagos blue butterfly

○ Galápagos puma

○ Galápagos hawk

Like most Galápagos animals, these sea lions aren't afraid of people.

We're lucky to be visiting this beautiful place, so we SHOULD treat it with respect.

Protected islands

There are many rules in place to protect the Galápagos Islands and their wildlife. Can you spot FOUR rule-breakers on this beach?

Night visions

Around the world, people gazing at the full Moon imagine pictures
in the dark, patch-like craters that cover its surface.

Look at the examples at the bottom
of the page. Then, if you can
see any different pictures, draw
their outlines here.

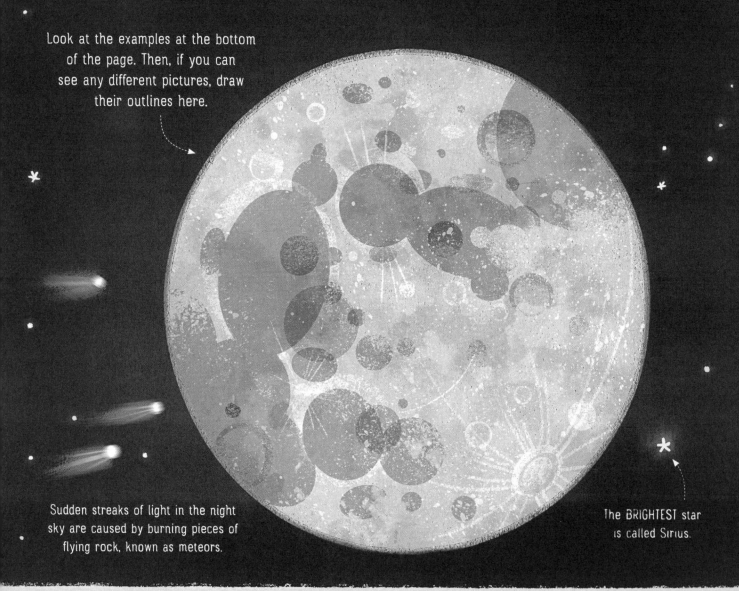

Sudden streaks of light in the night
sky are caused by burning pieces of
flying rock, known as meteors.

The BRIGHTEST star
is called Sirius.

Rabbit mashing rice
(East Asia)

Face
(North America)

Handprints
(India)

Man carrying sticks
(Europe)

Sky lights and shapes

Shimmering pink, purple and green lights sometimes brighten the sky near the North and South Poles.

Circle every fifth letter on this picture to spell out their scientific name.

L K P D A M R Y W U P D X I R Q M E P O L J C U R O F W L A

Types of birds called starlings fly in great, shape-shifting groups above parts of Europe.

Did you know there's a word for a flock of starlings? If you replace each of these letters with the one before it in the alphabet, you'll find the word.

N V S N V S B U J P O

....

Rainbows appear when sunlight shines through tiny drops of water in the air.

```
1 8 4 3 9 A 3 6 2 8 3 L 3 6 7 2 3 M 5 2 4 6 7 8 9 O 9 2 3 S 5 9 3 T 2 6 7 8 9
  2 3 7 5 9 6 4 2 5 6 4 T 5 2 2 A 9 5 3 8 T 2 6 7 3 E 8 9 2 5 3 O 3 4 2 F 6 4
    3 5 8 2 4 3 A 6 3 9 2 5 4 P 7 8 4 6 5 P 3 6 2 6 4 9 E 2 3 5 7 A 2 6 R 9 5
      4 7 5 9 I 5 2 3 7 8 N 6 2 3 5 T 8 9 2 3 H 6 4 5 2 E 7 2 1 6 U 7 2 5 3 S 2
        9 3 R 6 7 2 5 A 4 3 9 I 2 6 4 N 6 6 8 3 B 4 9 3 6 2 O 8 3 5 W 4 6 2 S
          5 3 H 9 5 4 7 2 4 3 A 2 4 6 5 3 W 9 4 6 2 3 A 6 4 2 9 8 I 2 3 6 7 I 8
            4 6 3 E 2 9 8 5 6 V 2 3 E 7 7 9 R 8 4 4 5 2 Y 3 9 D 8 2 4 A 6 4 Y 3
```

There's a fact hidden on this rainbow's stripes. First, cross out any numbers (1-9), then look at the letters on each stripe, from left to right, following the order of the key. Write the letters in the spaces below.

KEY

_ _ _ _ _ _ _ _ _ _ _ _ _ _ _ _

_ _ _ _ _ _ _ _ _ _ _ _ _ _ _ _ _

_ _ _ _ _ _ _ _ _ _ _ _ _ _ _ _ _ _

SAVE THE PLANET

People cause most of the problems facing Planet Earth.
BUT they can also help to fix them...

Finding solutions

Can you pair up the Earth-friendly ideas under the five pictures
with the different problems on the yellow signs?

1. Turning the water off
when you brush your teeth

◯ Throwing things away after
using them ONLY once

Lots of the things that people
throw away are buried under the
ground or burned. This poisons
the ground and the air.

2. Picking up litter
on beaches

◯ Transporting food VERY
long distances

3. Reusing and recycling
things as much as possible

◯ Driving cars

Engines release gases
that harm the planet's
protective atmosphere.

4. Walking or cycling
whenever possible

◯ Dumping plastic
into the seas

◯ Wasting water

It takes lots of energy to
make water safe to use.

5. Eating food grown
locally if you can

Clean energy

More and more countries around the world are using the Earth's natural forces to produce energy – instead of burning dirty fuels.

Write the letters A–D on the posters, to show in which place each of these types of clean energy technology could be used best.

A. Strong winds spin turbines to make electricity.

B. Geothermal pumps collect hot water from deep underground. They use it to make energy.

C. Water flows through hydroelectric dams to generate electricity.

D. Solar panels turn sunlight into energy.

Welcome to
Nizwa, Oman

Don't forget your shades!

You'll be blown away by

Barrow Island, Australia

STEAM VALLEY
ICELAND

VISIT OUR NATURAL HOT SPRINGS.

Africa's
Zambezi River

BEWARE of the fast-flowing rapids!

Under protection

Over 200,000 places on Earth are so IMPORTANT for wildlife that they're protected by law. These places are known as protected areas.

Can you fill in the letters missing from the names of seven protected areas on the right? You'll find all these places in this book.

1. G _ _ AT B _ R _ _ E _ R _ E _

2. A _ T _ RC _ _ _ A

3. _ R _ _ D C _ NY _ _

4. M _ RI _ _ _ A _ R _ N _ H

5. GA _ Á _ _ G _ S I _ _ A _ D _

6. I _ U _ Z _ F _ _ L _

7. M _ _ NT _ IL _ _ A _ J _ _ O

59

SPREAD THE WORD

One way that you can help to save the planet is to speak up about its problems and let people know what they should do.

Can you complete the slogans on the top three signs?
Choose which words to write on each one.

...to save our seas.   ...by unplugging them!   ...into treasure.

SLAY ENERGY VAMPIRES...

....
....

Devices that drain power – even when they're switched off – are known as energy vampires.

Transform your trash...

....
....

Say NO to plastic...

....
....

Now, make up designs and your own slogan for these signs, too.

Protect Earth's wildlife.

Adopt a polar bear TODAY!

....
....

....

Plant more trees to keep the Earth GREEN!

ANSWERS AND SOLUTIONS

4-5 INSIDE AND OUTSIDE THE EARTH

Surface spotting:
A. ☐ B. ☐ C. ☐
D. ☑ E. ☐ F. ☐

Hidden layers:
1. Inner core
2. Outer core
3. Mantle
4. Crust

Up in the air:
A. Thermosphere, B. Mesosphere, C. Troposphere,
D. Stratosphere, E. Exosphere

6-7 DIFFICULT DESERTS

Saharan survivors:
1. D, 2. C, 3. A, 4. B

Count the arms:
From left to right, number the cacti:
4, 3, 8, 6, 2, 5, 1, 7.

Desert bloom:
1. B9, 2. G1, 3. E4,
4. F7, 5. A3

From flower to flower:
A. 2, B. 4, C. 3, D. 6, E. 5
Insect D visited the most flowers.

8-9 WONDERFUL WATERFALLS

Waterfall search:

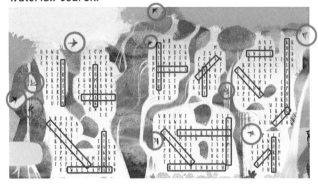

Record breakers:
From left to right, the waterfalls
are 18, 10, 3 and 16.

Spot the swifts:
There are ten swifts.

10-11 SKY-SCRAPING MOUNTAINS

Higher and higher:
Number the mountains from left to right:
6, 7, 3, 4, 2, 1, 5.

Back to the woods:

Cold at the top:

12-13 SURGING SEAS

Big waves:

RUEGOWVAEORGE
OUEGRVAEWRUGEOWVAE
GROEUEVAWRGUCEEWAVUR
REUGOAWVEGROEUAVERO
WORRUEAGOUEVAVAEWRU
WOGRUEAVOUEGRVAEWRUG
REUGOAWVEGROEUAVEROU
WOGRUEAVOUEGRVAEWRUGE
REUGOAWVEGROEUAVEROGEU
RWOGRUEAVOUEGRVAEWRUGEO
REUGOAWVE*GROGUEWAVE*ROGERO
RWOGRUEAVOUEGRVAEWRUGEWAVREO

Lost city:
◯ Nine gold coins   ◯ Two statues   ◯ Six clay pots

Track the ducks:
The currents lead to:
1. Europe, 2. North America,
3. South America, 4. Australasia, 5. Asia

Turning tides:
High tide
reaches line B.

14-15 ALL SORTS OF CITIES

Skyline shapes:
A. Cape Town
B. Carcassonne
C. Tampa
D. La Paz
E. Manila
F. Sydney

Two-wheel tour:

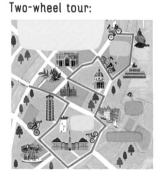

16-17 THE GREATEST JOURNEYS ON EARTH

On the move:
There are 29 zebras, 26 wildebeest and 26 gazelles,
so there are more zebras.
There are five hidden leopards.

Lost fawns:

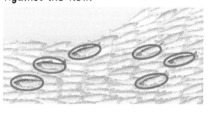

Tracking birds:
A. Blue grouse
B. Eurasian crane
C. Arctic tern

Against the flow:

18-19 TANGLED MANGROVES

Protective plants:
There are 16 fish.

Whose roots?:
1. B, 2. C, 3. A

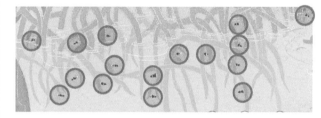

Plastic problem:
There are nine bottles and eight bags.
The volunteers need three sacks.

20-21 THE ICY NORTH AND SOUTH

Cracks in the ice:

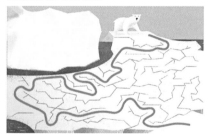

Tip of the iceberg:
Add...
1. Two squares above
2. 35 squares below
3. Four squares above
4. 21 squares below
5. Seven squares above

Southern stations:
The South Pole is here.

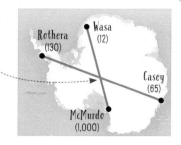

22-23 THE AMAZING AMAZON

Layers of life: One malachite butterfly is missing.

What's that flower?:
Label the flowers from left to right:
3, 4, X, 5, 2, 1.
The third flower doesn't match a description.

Monkey maze:

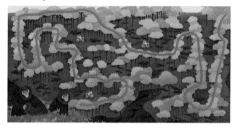

24-25 FROZEN FORESTS

Tough trees:
There are 35 spruce, 42 pine and 43 larch trees.

Beware of the bogs: **Taiga tiger:**

Camp conversation:
Label the translations from top to bottom: D, A, B, C.

26-27 THE RING OF FIRE

Mapping volcanoes:

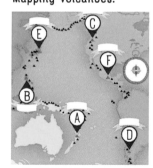

Timeline:
The order of the volcanoes is
E, F, D, A, B, C.

Eruption report:
The missing details appear
in this order from top
to bottom:
8:32am, ash, sky,
stream, speed.

Race to the top:
A. 5 hours 30 minutes, B. 7 hours 45 minutes,
C. 6 hours 30 minutes
The climber should choose Route A.

28-29 DEEP UNDERGROUND

Strange names:

Cave bacon:

Soda straws:

Cave popcorn:

Cave frostwork:

Crystal cave:

30-31 EXTREME WEATHER

Drifting dust:
Picture C

How much hail?:
132 days of hail

Wet season sudoku:

32-33 RECORD-BREAKING LANDMARKS
Wish you were where?: Eden Project

34-35 THE GRAND CANYON

Camera angles: The picture was taken by Rosa.

Lizard lookout:

Star spotting:
◯ Orion's Belt   ◯ Rigel   ◯ Venus   ◯ Betelgeuse

36-37 ISLANDS IN THE SEAS
Largest islands:
Greenland - 42, Sumatra - 9, Honshu - 5, Madagascar - 11,
Baffin Island - 10, Borneo - 15, New Guinea - 16
Together, New Guinea, Borneo and Madagascar are the
same size as Greenland.

Land of lemurs:
There are 18 ring-tailed lemurs, 11 sifakas, 13 aye-ayes
and 14 red ruffed lemurs.

Appearing and disappearing:

Artificial islands:
1. D, 2. C, 3. A, 4. B

38-39 SPRAWLING SAVANNAHS

Elephant gardeners:

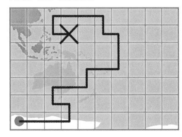

Up in flames:
Cross out these facts:
★ Lightning never
  causes wildfires.
★ Wildfires only happen
  in Australasia.

42-43 DEEP UNDERWATER

Find the trench:

Venting letters:
BLACK SMOKERS

Glowing in the dark:
1. Deep-sea dragonfish
2. Crossota jellyfish
3. Firefly squid
4. Black seadevil
5. Hatchetfish

Journey to the bottom:
The missing times are 7:52am, 10:52am, 12:02pm.

44-45 FEEDING THE PLANET

Copy cow:

The great fish escape: Seven salmon have escaped.

Collecting cane:
Fill in these numbers and
directions from top to bottom:
2, 6, left, 2, left, 5, right, 1.

Busy bees:
The hive should
go in field D.

46-47 THE GREAT LAKES

Route finder:

True or false?:
1. False
2. True
3. False
4. False
5. True

Superior sketches: Sketch B is the closest match.

48-49 THE GREAT BARRIER REEF

How many reefs?:
2,900 reefs make up the Great Barrier Reef.

Which fish?:
The order of the fish is 3, 4, 2, 1.

50-51 QUAKING EARTH

Plates puzzle:

Find the faults:
1. San Andreas Fault
2. Mid-Atlantic Ridge
3. Pacific-Antarctic Ridge

Rippling out:
The earthquake will reach the places in this order: 2, 1, 4, 3, 5.

Quake-proof towers:
TORRE REFORMA, TOKYO SKYTREE, SHANGHAI TOWER, TRANSAMERICA PYRAMID, BURJ KHALIFA

52-53 WORLD OF WONDERS

Visit Blood Falls:
B. Lots of iron

Scale giant steps:

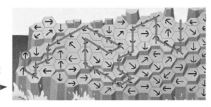

54-55 TORTOISE ISLANDS

Island hopping:
Route C suits all three tourists.

Darwin's journey:
Darwin visited these islands in this order: San Cristóbal, Floreana, Isabela and Santiago.

Real or fake?:
Label the animals from left to right: D, C, B, X, A. The Galápagos puma isn't real.

Protected islands:

56-57 LOOKING UP FROM EARTH

Sky lights and shapes:
The lights' scientific name is AURORA.
A flock of starlings is called a MURMURATION.
The fact hidden in the stripes is: RAINBOWS APPEAR ALMOST EVERY DAY IN THE US STATE OF HAWAII.

58-59 SAVE THE PLANET

Finding solutions:
1. Wasting water, 2. Dumping plastic into the seas, 3. Throwing things away after using them ONLY once, 4. Driving cars, 5. Transporting food VERY long distances

Clean energy:
A. Barrow Island
B. Steam Valley
C. Zambezi River
D. Nizwa

Under protection:
1. GREAT BARRIER REEF, 2. ANTARCTICA, 3. GRAND CANYON, 4. MARIANA TRENCH, 5. GALÁPAGOS ISLANDS, 6. IGUAZÚ FALLS, 7. MOUNT KILIMANJARO

60 SPREAD THE WORD

Transform your trash into treasure.
Say no to plastic to save our seas.
Slay energy vampires by unplugging them!

Additional writing by Jordan Akpojaro and Matthew Oldham

Additional illustrations by Lucy Semple

Additional design by Tom Lalonde and Claire Morgan

Series editor: Jane Chisholm   Series designer: Helen Edmonds   Managing designer: Zoe Wray   Digital manipulation by John Russell